NEW WINGS

D1076785

Robyn Bolam was born in Newcastle, and grew up in Northumberland. She has lived in Berkshire, Kent, Yorkshire, London and North-east Scotland. Her previous two collections, both published by Bloodaxe, appeared under her former married name, Marion Lomax: *The Peepshow Girl* (1989) and *Raiding the Borders* (1996). Her anthology *Eliza's Babes: four centuries of women's poetry in English* was published by Bloodaxe in 2005. Her latest selection *New Wings: Poems 1977-2007* (Bloodaxe Books, 2007) is a Poetry Book Society Recommendation.

In 1981, she received an Eric Gregory Award and won first prize in the Cheltenham Festival Poetry Competition. Her libretto for the opera *Beyond Men and Dreams* (composer Bennett Hogg) was performed by the Royal Opera House Garden Venture in 1991. She was awarded a Hawthornden International Fellowship in 1993, and held a British Council writing residency at the University of Stockholm in 1998. She has given readings of her poetry in Britain, Portugal, Sweden, Romania, USA and Japan.

ROBYN BOLAM

NEW WINGS

POEMS 1977-2007

BLOODAXE BOOKS

ISBN: 978 1 85224 778 2

First published 2007 by
Bloodaxe Books Ltd,
Highgreen,
Tarset,
Northumberland NE48 1RP.

www.bloodaxebooks.com
For further information about Bloodaxe titles
please visit our website or write to
the above address for a catalogue.

Bloodaxe Books Ltd acknowledges
the financial assistance of
Arts Council England, North East.

Cover design: Neil Astley & Pamela Robertson-Pearce.

Cover printing: J. Thomson Colour Printers Ltd, Glasgow.

Printed in Great Britain by
Bell & Bain Limited, Glasgow, Scotland.

CLEOPATRA: *If it be love indeed, tell me how much.*
ANTONY: *There's beggary in the love that can be reckoned.*
CLEOPATRA: *I'll set a bourn how far to be beloved.*
ANTONY: *Then must thou needs find out new heaven, new earth.*

William Shakespeare: *Antony and Cleopatra* (I.i. 14-17)

ACKNOWLEDGEMENTS

This book contains poems selected from two previous collections, *The Peepshow Girl* (1989) and *Raiding the Borders* (1996), both published by Bloodaxe Books under Robyn Bolam's former name, Marion Lomax.

Acknowledgements are due to the editors of the following publications in which eight of the *New Wings* new poems first appeared: *Interchange* (University of Wales, Aberystwyth, 1998), *New Writing, Poetry Review, Swedish Reflections: from Beowulf to Bergman* (Arcadia/British Council, 2003), and *The Tabla Book of New Verse, 1998*.

CONTENTS

FROM **THE PEEPSHOW GIRL** (1989)

11 The Forked Tree
12 Tenement Haiku
13 Passengers
14 Just Another Commuter
15 Blencathra
16 Tethera
17 Topsoil
18 The Hag's Daughter
18 Emily
19 Second Wife
20 Mrs Mackie
21 The Peepshow Girl
22 The American Bar
23 September 1943
24 Father Lofts Retires
24 Pheasants
25 Candles
26 Guardians
26 The Desk
27 Obsession
28 On Independence and Resolution
29 Second Honeymoon
30 A Jacobean Fragment
31 Isabelle of France
32 Ghosts

FROM **RAIDING THE BORDERS** (1996)

35 Kith
36 Compass
36 Between Voyages
37 Sealing
38 First Lessons
39 Somewhere Else
40 Gruoch Considers
40 Gruoch
41 The Boatman's Dream
42 Dead Books [2]
42 Mixed Doubles
43 Beyond Men
44 Quaking Houses

46 Raiding the Borders
48 Special Delivery
49 Amor Diving
50 The First Week
51 Post-natal
52 The Day of the Funeral
53 The Other Itinerary
54 Left Luggage
55 July
56 Gulf
57 Difficult Times
58 Divided We Stand
59 God's Train
60 The Destruction of Sodom and Gomorrah
62 Pandora's Daughter
63 Metaphor
64 Rock

NEW WINGS (1997-2007)
67 Strathieburn
68 Lifeblood
70 Learning to Read
71 Panoramic View
72 Signing Off
73 Two Springs
74 The Swedish Climate
74 Tobias and the Angel
76 Leonardo's Dog
77 Cacti and Love
78 For Eileen
79 Dream Lore
80 Meeting again after almost eight years
81 50s Jive
82 Kiss
83 The Attachment
84 Music of the Hemispheres
85 Wildfire
86 Mnemonic
88 Dreamcatcher
89 The Kiosk, Constanta
90 City Bride
91 Something Bigger
92 Through-lines

NOTES

FROM

The Peepshow Girl

(1989)

The Forked Tree

I killed two hares last night in the heart of the garden.
Long ears in moonlight, mimicking the shape of the tree.
I crept round the side of the house before they sensed me
And when they heard the gun clear its throat it was too late.
I hit the buck first, then the doe – stupidly standing
To stare at me. Her powerful hindquarters refusing
To kick and run, though I knew she could have bounded up
The lane in an instant, back to her young. I can cope
With hares: they are easy to cook. I feel no remorse.
Now I'll wait for the vixen who raids the chicken house.

I feed my chickens. Gather and sort the eggs. I wipe
The dirt and straw collage from the shells of those I sell.
I have the dogs too. My husband trained them, but I was
Surprised how quickly they obeyed me. I talked to them –
More easily than I talked to the children. Could share
The shadow with its dark gun lurking by our house wall
And the silent bullet lodged inside before we knew
That it was growing. His coming out of hospital,
Then the sniper's second strike when he was off his guard.
In the end I could only stand stupidly and stare –

Even with warning, could not believe such treachery.
The children were swinging from the tree in the garden
With no one to catch them. Darkness made the ground tremble
With hooves which left the grass trampled and the roses spoiled.
I guard this warren – small rooms and scattered outbuildings.
Not even chickens shall live in fear of predators.
My children shall feed better than before. Lonely nights
Are not without fear, but I cope with darkness now that
I have seen it bring young deer down from the wood to play,
Jumping in and out in the moonlight, through the forked tree.

Tenement Haiku

In a spacious room
A girl plays a violin
Rephrasing her youth.

The women work on
Straining to hear a distant
And difficult tune.

Passengers

An old woman sifts through sepia prints,
Photographs and faded postcards –
Regards a picture of herself as a girl
Sitting stiff-backed in an Edwardian hat.
The curve of her cheek, flawless skin,
Lips pertly pressed, and the profile
Of her breasts beneath those crisp pleats,
That tight bodice and high neck.

Moving back behind the glass
Into the insect-laden dusk
Her skirt sweeps the veranda steps.
Babies sleep under mosquito nets –
The rockers scrape; she hears the veld
Softly dousing the sunbird's breast
And as her lips remember it
She tips the starlings' wings with red.

Day brings the boy with a pony and trap:
She clambers up – sets off alone.
Beneath her veil she feels the rain
Gather to obscure the view, as locusts did
That afternoon the sky went black.
Too soon, out here, the gullies fill
And wash you down: she cracks the whip.
A whistle sounds across the veld.

The day they came from Pietermaritzburg
He smoked with the guard and held her glove.
Now she rides the long mountain train
That twists like a snake and steeply turns
Till the room shudders to a wrinkled hand.
A bemused passenger, she rubs the glass
Of the last carriage; looking back –
At herself, staring forward in the first.

Just Another Commuter

Two seats in front: just out of reach
As the bus lurches on I stare
At his back and his old black jacket
Worn light in places, bagging with age.
I see the space where his workbag
Pressed his shoulder, and growing bolder
I look into the dark window
And try to see his face, but his neighbour
Is nearer and hides him from view.

From here he could well be my father,
But rather than make, what can only be
An embarrassing mistake, I sit until
We reach our destination. His thinning hair
Has one side brushed over;
I wonder if he will still know me –
Remembering him too well, I don't feel
So much older. We reach the terminus
And he is still too far to touch.

I know it is a futile hope – not having
Seen him for so long, but foolish thoughts
Haunt as we move down. He turns. One glance
Changes the familiar frame into a stranger.
I had always known it would be so, yet
Did not know which was the worst to bear –
The disappointment I felt at being left,
Or the relief at being spared
Seeing a dead man walk towards the stairs.

Blencathra

The sky is like nothing else in the garden –
Cornflower, delphinium, nor campanula.
Spokes of lavender wheel it round. I sit here
So pain can watch it seed clouds, tease them out
Into faces which start to say something
Then dissolve. It forms mountains on air
Supporting each other: a balance of vapour.
It has walled in the world with a hard blue –
No gaps. Clouds to the fore, it slides past slowly,
An unbroken belt. We rest against it
Moving closer: night tightens its notch.

As a child, when relatives died, I searched
For their features in the clouds. Not long ago
My father smiled above Blencathra. You say
You cannot bear to lose me to the weather.
My love, I would stay up here forever, where
An invisible tide turns in the trees,
Church bells are silent in the valley and shreds
Of tattered rope float out like hands through
The slatted tower: time must be slower.
Streams flow down the mountain; somewhere
An old glacier is still coldly melting.

In this high place the sky has quiet power –
Strolling through the house opening up windows.
My face pressed to the landscape of your chest
We share an internal world of stars – when I ache
You bury me under a weight of sky to wake smiling.
Other nights my features vaporise, look down
On you, alone in a borrowed garden,
Where the sky supported our sheltered dreams.
The city forces us to speak less, think more –
Restless against a blue, paler than eyes,
Wearied by hoardings that never stop talking.

Tethera

Yan, tan, tethera, methera
CUMBRIAN SHEPHERD COUNT

Always the third sheep to be counted.
They came struggling out of the water,
Shook themselves like huge dogs on the beach,
Ignored our fires and took to the hills
As that first wreck swept under the waves:
Screams are the same in any language.
For many shapes of the moon the sea
Washed ashore men's bodies. We left them
In the shallow caves then moved inland.
Sea – a thin blue line from the mountain
When low clouds pass. We did not go back.

Sheep graze slate-lined streets: steady workers –
The persistent rasp of savaged grass
Has come to soothe us. They move heads down,
Their backs like dirty, leftover snow.
Wool nests collect, blow into gullies.
New lambs squeeze in between the tree roots,
Heads wedged against the trunk, out of the wind
Which chartered this city; set statutes
For a shepherd people who see life
Always at an angle; whose stories
Fell from fleeces, damp and heavy with weed.

Swifts flit in and out where the mountain
Allowed our forefathers to enter.
We gather crooked spires of foxgloves,
Strip leaves to make the heart beat slower,
Keep a pulse beaten by the weather.
Most valleys now think us legend.
Down there a cow walks across a field
Surprisingly quickly, smaller than
A brown bead of dung. We feel rain nip.
Change will come with their disenchantment,
Bringing them here – yan, tan, tethera –
Eager to mate with our daughters and sons.

16

Topsoil

I walk these moors for what they are.
The wind's runways. It swoops
Whoo-ing in my ears like sad owls,
Their beaks at my face where
The scarf can't cover. Beyond them
Curlews, constantly panicking,
Calling away from invisible nests.

This is the sky's full drop.
It doesn't have to cramp around cities
Or spear itself on spires.
Here it can stretch down its legs
And walk. It strides over the heather
Farther than I can see. The curlews
Call between its knees.

I walk these moors for what they are.
Neglected roof gardens of the mill towns
Left to fend for themselves, riding
The landscape with a small burden of sheep
And Sunday walkers. Where purple flowers
Tongue a late summer bell
Pealing low blue notes.

The marsh sucks my feet to a certain depth
And no further. The old sheep tracks lie
Deep down with monks' footprints.
Below, an Iron Age prospector once scratched
For ore, plundered trees for his furnace,
And below, a Bronze Age shepherd
Slept beneath them.

It matters little that the Vikings came
Or the Romans landed. That once this
Vast scar of heath was solid ice
Or fertile forest. The peat preserves
Old seeds: all swallowed now and
Well digested. I walk these moors
For what they are.

The Hag's Daughter

Behind the church a limestone well
Drips persistently on an old doll
Left long ago to be turned to stone
By her mother's so-called sorcery.

An old woman now, she has back-packed
Her hump between the houses
For eighty years. She never shared
Her mother's indifference to these people.

Still they turn away in the street.
Kindly enough, but reluctant to stand
Long in her gaze – as if afraid that
The sediment in her eyes may petrify.

Emily

I don't know how they dared
Put you under the pavement
In the family vault when
There was so much moor.

Even the graveyard is more
Akin, its strict boundaries
Holding back a silent
Clamour of escaped

Weeds and tangled flowers
Moving wildly in the wind.
You'd frown to see the crowds
Flocking to the house

Convinced they sense your spirit
In the reconstructed kitchen.
It's almost as naïve
As those good churchmen

Believing that you'd let them
Tuck you safely into dust.
It suggests great folly, or
Even greater trust.

Second Wife

This house with a past is appropriate.
Each of us is new only to the other;
We all lived with someone else
Before we finally came together.

You talk of years in empty rooms,
Of a garden – like this one – gone to seed.
Nettles and honeysuckle choking in turn;
Sharp-beaked birds nesting in the weed.

I gouge out roots and clear the stones.
Work hard, but grow disturbed to find –
Beneath the weeds a pattern shows
Which, earlier, someone else designed.

Mrs Mackie

Thor's a netty in the kitchen
Ahint that door: waal's a bit femma.
Roond heyor, most fowk
Gan in the yard – cistin is
Alwis freezin' up and ye cud
Breck yor neck on them stairs
Oot the back – twenty-fower –
Aa coonted them mesel
Day w' moved in. Had te lug
The dressor up wiv a rope.
Wad he' smashed te smithereens
If the lads doonstairs
Hadn't ev held it. Me man's muthor's –
Dark oak – a deed weight.
Aa've alwis hoovered roond it.
Divvent knaa hoo aa'll tyek it oot.
Sh' shud've put w' in
A proper bathroom
But sh' knaaed sh'd nivvor
Get owt back on the rent.
Just shut the door
When ye de yor dinnor.
The front winder wants a shove –
Sash is brokken, but the road's
Ower mucky anyways
And the buses myek it rattle.
Divvent gan an faall
Doon the stairs – oil-cloth's ripped.
If the sink clogs up, nivvor worry –
It gans doon slaa lyke.
Aa's not keen te gan ye knaa,
Divvent think it.
If aa cud get aroond
Withoot this soddin' frame
Ye waddent hev a chance
Of a playce lyke this.

The Peepshow Girl

Amongst the long grass
Of downtown Berlin
Manet settles
Behind shutter five
And begins to sketch.

She flexes her back,
Turns on a stare.
Other shutters shoot up.
She rotates – her back
Curved to Picasso –

She knows that Degas
Is watching her legs.
Coins fall through the slots.
The shutters shoot up
For a minute; clatter down.

Her limbs drift through postures:
The minutes fall.
She will leave fully clothed –
A throng already gathering
For the next session –

Take the U-Bahn with tourists,
Schoolboys out after hours,
The unmarriageable, the deserted,
The curious street artist –
Disquieting them with avid eyes.

The American Bar

Saturday night in the American sector.
A few lonely faces at empty tables –
Bespectacled boys with short hair and Stetsons
Plucking the gingham cloths with thin fingers.
And the rest of the tables over-heavy
With whooping GIs and Berlin women
Shrieking for burgers and Southern Comfort.

Joe tries to pull his sweat-shirt over his stomach
And stretches to put on another record.
Between the tables and the bar they shuffle
Along the edges of a clumsy square dance.
Mothered by kisses and manicured hands:
New York, Kentucky, L.A. – hemming in
A square of stained floor-boards in West Berlin.

September 1943

Dear _____

The trains help the night keep time; marking certain minutes past
And on the hour. My dreams align with them, rushing the dark.
Locked in our different compartments with empty carriages
Between us – we do not meet. I see us hurtling through
The bombed remains of cities. Each station a gaping hole
Where the platform dropped away; where the train can never stop.

There were no windows in the truck which you were forced to board
While they brought me on here by road with the other women
To these lines of squat huts where we work or lie and listen
To the trains entering the tunnels of our sleeping heads.
Each night is spent trying to roll the heavy door across
And run back down the track, hoping to find you before light.

Morning swoops down, gold on its talons, clawing up new sounds
To drown the noise of trains. They make us clap back the shutters,
Strip us of our dreams. My rough hands cling to keep them draped
          here
Across these windows glaring starkly over empty beds.
There is an ache behind my eyes when I put my weight to
The unyielding door, and feel only the creak of the sky.

Years ago, in another country, I saw an eagle
Fly between two mountains, its wings sweeping gold on the sea.
My father put aside our old troubles and exulted:
'They that wait upon the Lord shall renew their strength; they shall
Mount up with wings as eagles; shall run and not be weary.'
Lately, I have heard his voice more clearly; just as I wake.

Father Lofts Retires

It was not lightly done to sacrifice
People for the small-talk of flowers;
Count purlins and rafters swelling with rain;
To sleep in a house starting to grow again.
Creeping branches had lifted gutters;
Ivy made its way through the walls,
And the earth oozed with unknown wells.

Ashamed, he did not miss parishioners' feet
On the hollow stairs, or the vast back room
Where he took his meals. There was more life
In the squabbling birds, and sheep
Occasionally raising a senile cheer,
Than he had ever known in the gaunt manse
With its curtains falling on bended knee.

Pheasants

The colour of paths: a dull, speckled brown.
I watched her cross the gravel by the door;
Circumnavigate the lawn, breast-high in grass.
A dowdy bird with the wind up her skirts,
Lifting fans of feathers as she strutted –
Out on her own as the air shook with rain.

In green balaclava and red face mask
Her mate invaded through a hole in the hedge.
Rain glistened on his copper, black-ribbed back;
On the metallic tan of breast and tail –
Tipped upright in the wind, like a hat.
A chauvinist bird (in the modern sense)

He insisted on following her around –
Half-raising her wings to the daffodils
She hid among the flowers' yellow heads
While he peered, parrot-like. At last she fled
But froze in her tracks at his harsh, throaty cry
And turned back as if resigned to her lot.

Then, freedom meant to the end of the hedge
Or a few minutes by the magnolia tree.
Two days later, she was hit by a car
And died more dramatically than she lived –
Since when, he has paced this short lane – nagged
By her new independence, and more rain.

Candles

We burn them for love – a man on Skye poured
The purple of the mountains into sand
Near a narrow loch visited by whales.
Beyond three rowan trees the sea grew tame
And nightly he would light the floating dark.

Beside the bed, this pool of wax in sand
Melts walls to make an island estuary.
New tides rib the sheets; damp bodies poured
Relax the skin of mountains, taut before
The warm loch lured the leviathan.

Guardians

The roses will be heavy now at Foxhill;
They bear the house down towards the lake
And the vast rooms where we used to live
Will stare as sunlight hesitates.

I remember the sound of the bird trapped
To flap all night in the panelled room,
How bats and stars sparkled in the stained glass
And windows flew open in the rain.

The swans will come back to nest and feed,
Children litter the lawn with their debris
And from this far garden I have decreed
New lovers to gather on the fallen tree.

The Desk

It stood in the corner of the shop window
Carrying fifty-six inches of ship, aground
On its walnut surface, swirling with dust.
The four drawers on either side were false:
They swung open together like ships' lockers;
But the one in the centre was real and rasped
When it moved along a sanded slipway.
More than I could afford, but I bought it anyway,
And a man in a shabby jerkin removed the ship,
Casting the desk off without a cargo.

I anchored it between the shutters of this window.
The wasteland yaws between glass and sky.
Hands of red and green Virginia creeper
Reach wetly over the top of a wall.

It has rained ever since I left my old city;
The tide goes out through four lanes of traffic,
Beacons flashing at the end of the street.
The desk is loaded with papers, spilling over.
I float here charting a way to evening –
Leaving black lines in the wake of my pen.

Obsession

Days pass as dreams: he never wakes
From the rattle of the needle –
Day after day he sews vast wings.
Josepha squeezes between bales
Of tough white sail-cloth as she sings.

Meals come on a reach – up the stairs:
He stitches panels into place.
Her arm, a boom across his thoughts,
Thrusts down the tray. Her oiled black hair
Swings like a rope out of his grasp.

She makes him polish brown-grained knees,
Her white blouse ripples from beneath.
He notices her feet are wet
Starts to take stock of her veneer
Is stopped – and does what she suggests.

He plays her hair out through his hands
Watches her artful practised arch.
She smiles – he strokes her varnished legs;
Sighs – he will turn away from land
And haul the white blouse to her neck.

On Independence and Resolution

The man next door snores in Portuguese.
He keeps me awake all night, then doesn't speak
When he hands me your letter in the morning.
What would be the point? I could only smile
Like a door closing quietly, if he did.

Bells drag their shadows across the sand
To a glimmer of children. You will not know
The pain I feel when I read her name
Mentioned carelessly, so many times.
I will wish you both well and send my love.

Some nights I dream of what led me here; how I feared
The woman who walked up a road to a shuttered house.
I love the wind chimes of rigging in the harbour:
When the tide comes in, the sea is always warmer;
And your smile does not curve into a key.

Second Honeymoon

Only one of us arrived at the old hotel.
Madame unlocked the door to stale air,
Apologetic walls. Alone, my tightly fitting toe
Teased the slight tear in a damp sheet
Among corridors of vacated rooms
Window bills murmuring *A Vendre*.

Rain made the dining room a candled cave.
Maids draped with coats ran to bring brooms
And swilled it through the aisles into the street.
At another stranded table, a woman sat
Dressed for herself, reading a book,
Absorbed in the place's tender despair.

The top storey shutters were battened down.
No one seemed to come or go, yet there was
A light at the top of the stairs
As if someone was quietly remembering
Cars cruising in, a volley of corks, the din –
White cloths piled high with fruits de mer.

In the night the sea rolled up over the road
Whipping pebbles at windscreens, chipping wings.
This morning, below the peeling shutters,
Cars seem shocked, gritted with gravel, barnacles
On their salt-stained tyres; seaweed exhausts.
Severed tentacles smear the lobby floor.

Today the light rings silver, off-key.
Madame sits by the door with tightly clenched fists
While men she might once have invited in
Shoulder heirlooms past her tired legs.
The road is strewn with shells and hollow crabs:
I cross a livid tidemark; scattered sand.

A Jacobean Fragment

I am a dagger in
A dark corner
Searing silk.

I am the layer of
Dust on a
Poisoned book.

I deal in distortion:
Voices reverse
In me. I speak

Through shadows
Live in echoes
Feed on both

Kinds of oblivion:
Love. Death. They
Couple in my kiss.

Performance is all.
Juggler of
Memento mori

I gore silence
Dip my hands
In it gleefully.

Smother candles
Squeeze night's throat
To vomit diamonds.

My breath is close
Smells of sweetmeats
And dry earth.

I grin across the ages
Moon's skull in
A clouded sky.

Isabelle of France

Ineluctable:
The rain drips
Like a clock
In this quiet house.

Love is a strange brooch –
I will grow old here
Among the fruit trees,
Mending my jewellery

Letting these eaves birds
Scrabble at my heart.
Butterflies, bruised flowers:
Stoical roses.

Light stirs the garden –
A foreign country.
No chance of meeting
Anyone I know.

The eloquent rain
Wakes me with stories,
Told through centuries
Of roses and snow.

Ghosts

In her dream she woke as usual;
The bed felt softer than she remembered.
Her head did not turn easily
And something was sitting on her feet
But this ceased to worry her.
The room felt full of people.

It often happened in this house –
Usually they didn't stay too long
Sometimes didn't properly form
But she preferred it when they did.
Ghosts with faces were more
Interesting. They had faces now.

They had surprised her at times
Where she least expected them
But in all these years
Had never come into this room
Till now. These seemed quite
Different. More substantial.

She found their macabre eyes
Disconcerting. They seemed
To hover round the bed.
She was sure they were talking.
Though she had sensed conversation
They had never spoken before.

They were moving closer. Becoming
Clearer. She did not know them.
Their faces swivelled.
One drew the curtain.
Another lifted the sheet
To her face.

Raiding the Borders

(1996)

Kith

On the other side of the border
they call this *Scozia Irredenta*:
unredeemed.
     A few coffers of coins
didn't change hands; a battle was lost
instead of won; the in-between land
stays in-between.
     A line on a map
moved back through the years
          down to the Tees.
England was never an only child
but has grown to think so. Stone streets dip –
rise. They're burning coal on morning fires
in dark front rooms: smoke gusts over roofs.
Gardens, late coming into flower,
brazen it out with bright aubrietia.

I've followed the hills to Carter Bar
past lost peels, and moors where soaking sheep
stagger between tufts of died-back grass.
Standing in the rain, she's there – harassed,
hurt – a foster-mother, telling me
she hasn't much to offer. I'll take
my chance: I don't believe her.
          The bends
on the border
          won't make up their minds.
Five times
          they twist me round, but I still
head north.

Compass

From the back yard look across the valley:
the Tyne winds east past castle and factory,
imperceptibly tidal. If you live
here long enough you learn to sense changes
as surreptitious as the river's ebb.

Once it was easier to keep your bearings –
the West Road to Hexham, the old East School;
though I lived in South Road the view was north,
child and woman before me would look up,
eyes drawn over fields to the Cheviots.

We were rivers who flowed from west to east,
to work and school, who faced north when we stopped
because it was known. Yet at our backs there was
always the south, enjoying the most sun,
making the needle quiver, faces turn.

Between Voyages

You brought me a seahorse, succulent shells.
The boat in the garden nudges the hedge;
its shrouds call up storms and a distant sea
where people, like sails, flap impatiently
with the pain of the land-bound watching tides.

Rain skitters down tiles: the gutters have gone.
Water flows below floors, rises up through
the ground floating spring bulbs and snails; their shells
striped whorls, brittle as memories of your voice –
close as the cold day, dark as our lost north.

I savour the sea horse, stroke a starfish
I once found – stiff-fingered in the sea coal
of a wintered town. All day, through the house,
I have shells beneath my feet. The floors give
and flood, gulls wheel above this inland roof.

Sealing

(for my Arran cousins)

It is evening on Arran, antlers on a sky-line
as the mountain gathers its ridge of eyes, shy of us,
and soon gone – like this memory my mind fails to hold
four hundred miles south, far from the sea and scent of seals.

I am struggling free, feel the hard floor shrink to pebbles.
My feet deep in shingle, waves break on the other side
of the window, and I wait – wait until it seems that
the sea flows into a field, an edge of dry garden.

Then just when my soles sense the smoothness of boards, they slip
and I see the first dark head far out in the water –
another, another. I call them to swim closer
where roses bloom in plankton, to wash me from this room.

Before sand settles on a faded Persian carpet
a pup dives into its green and magenta. The wools
grow luminous underwater. Fish flick from nowhere
round my chair legs. Currents are colder than expected.

I swim off a shore-line sheltered by Kintyre: it is
late evening on Arran. I have been here a long time,
sleep seal sleep, swallow squid and eels – days brimming lust as
land trees ripen – watch humans safely from a distance.

First Lessons

I have learnt to walk
with fear on a leash:
it used to snarl at the door
every time I tried to leave.
Now it trots quietly
on impacted earth,
and sometimes it sleeps.

I'd forgotten how minds
can be open to the sky
with no overhanging boulders –
what it feels like to lie
stretched in damp, warm grass
with insects in my hair –
and the way you can hear
minute thrusts of plants.

I have perfected
throwing anger to gulls
who mew it back to sea,
and I marvel that sleep
saunters down from the high trees
to spirit you up there –
leaving the room without
opening a window.

Somewhere Else

When I phone part of me listens for home
hidden behind you: sometimes a cat purrs
from your knee. Here, you'll just hear my TV –
switched on so that something moves in the room.

We strangle feelings, squeezing them down wires.
My feet seek you in the night, my hands search
between cold sheets, and I wake confused with
windows in new places, the wardrobe moved.

Though not properly awake, already
I'm tuned in to the sound of distant planes.
As I staunch the sense of a severed self,
I feel you move silently, somewhere else.

Gruoch Considers

Dochter tae a king, faither sin taen,
mairrit, sin weeda. Aa dinna greet.
Ma lad, Lulach, maun gang hes ain gait
an gie's ane bricht chance tae lauch agin.
Nae weeda gin wife. Aa'm a steekit yett
sae bleth'rin gabs canna ca' 'Bizzem'.
It's sair ta dae – wha winna fa' whiles?
Aa'm youthfu' an maun hae a man sune
ellis ma saul sall skirl. Aa munna smuir.

MacBeathain cam yestreen. Dander lass,
ye winna swither an baith say ay.
Daith is aye ahint yon spaywife. Juist
tak wha ye wad – MacBeathain, Macbeth.

Gruoch

I have a name of my own. Gruoch –
a low growl of desire. He'd say it
and crush me against his throat. Gruoch –
his huge hands stroking my hip-length hair,
grasping it in his fists, drawing it taut
either side of my arms in ropes,
staked like a tent. He'd gasp when
folds slipped open, succulent
as split stems, to welcome him in.
How I held him, squeezed the sorrow
of no son out of him – for Lulach
was only mine, fruit of first union –
of Gillecomgain, forgotten by time.

He brought me Duncan as a trophy,
sweet revenge for my father's slaughter.
Upstarts never prosper. I was the true
King's daughter, Gruoch – uttered in wonder.
Seventeen years we reigned together through
keen seasons of hunger, feasting one to other.
War nor wantons wrenched him from me:
Gruoch – a whisper, sustaining fire.

He died before the battle with Malcolm:
obsequies cradled in a dry bed.
My mouth meandered down his body –
but it was winter, no bud stirring.
Gruoch – despairing: our death rattle.

The Boatman's Dream

Just a boatman's dream, the kid left behind –
flicking her damp dress round the staithes, salt-stained
where she wrung the corners out. Her mouth full
of sherbet and sailors' talk, bruising words
as she flings them – Mister, giv is a fish!
Me da's run off...'
                        He throws her mackerel,
five fish at her feet. She sits to pack them
slithering into her wide blue knickers.
Some are still gasping when she starts to run
home, past men watching another tide turn –
with the promise of unfamiliar sheets
and a younger woman to kiss them warm:

masts negotiate angles they can't keep.

Dead Books [2]

He won't remember the incident,
she doesn't recall the place – but they
were looking at a beautiful book
in a glass case. It was sad, he said,
the way both books and people could die
if they were no longer touched with love.
She left him to stay alive.

Mixed Doubles

If 'love' means 'nothing'
his smile has just caused her to
make a double fault.

Beyond Men

Through the shrunk boards
water strokes itself:
dives at the ends of staves.
Her eyes are out to sea:
she's gardening the waves,
weeding out boats before
they can put down roots.

Off the beach, women
bob like seals in their
round red caps – climb out,
and dance with strangers.

Under the pier, where
the sea has slipped back,
the wet sand is coldest.
It sucks her shoulders,
makes her shiver.
Arms, legs, breasts, slip
under: she struggles
out of the strong embrace.
Sleek, salt tongues of weed
lick neck and nipples –
waves return her hair
a tangle of black lace.

Dancers on the pier
drift home to their beds,
refusing late drinks
or a possessive caress.
Tonight the sea's moans
make women yearn
for something beyond
the love of men.

Quaking Houses
(in memory of Elizabeth and Arthur Gowland)

I still remember the sound of your laugh,
the lift of the latch; this is how lives pass.
There'd be a fire roaring in the range,
pans on trivets hissing into the flames,
and you'd roll a live coal across your hand
(underground, you'd nearly lost the whole arm):
'See this, pet!' 'Arthur, leave the bairn alone.'

Pit-wheel at the end of the street, high wall –
the same pit-head pool where you sat the night
my mother was born, keeping 'out the way'
as you'd been told. Listening to a vixen
bark across the fells, hunting for her young –
you thought of your hens, Lizzie's oaths, her moans.
Groped in the May dark for a woman's voice
that would let you go home. The midwife burnt
newspapers soaked in blood; you kissed Lizzie
on the lips, stroked my mother's face with a
finger betraying a trace of coal, though
you'd scrubbed your hands till they were almost raw.

She slept, your child; the house was quiet then.
Soon it quaked twice more with a mother's screams;
stairs and rooms strained as the three of them grew,
pounding the gently sinking floors; struggling
with doors that wouldn't close, dropped in their frames.
Windows stuck; the walls were shifting their weight
every time part of a ceiling collapsed
in a tunnel hundreds of feet beneath.

War lit its own fires, the sky flared for miles;
planes whined past: 'As if it's not worth bombing.'
Tending your allotment, feeding your hens,
you watched Italian prisoners cross the fells.
Just two of you now, you'd saved a few pounds
to move from the street to a 'proper' town
but Lizzie died of cancer – you'd retired.
Silicosis, heart; you had a few years.

44

The houses? Modernised, without the mine,
they're still standing firm at thousands a time –
I can hear you laugh. This is how lives pass.

Raiding the Borders

Limmer thieves from robber towers,
the reivers rode after Lammas
when nights were longest, horses stronger.
Sometimes those they sought to plunder
saw the fires lit in warning,
heard the fray bell, were prepared.

Centuries later feuds were buried,
families allied to survive.
As my mother met my father,
back through the Bolams and the Halls,
Rutherfords, and Burnses further north –
marriages crossed over borders.

When they came down from the shires
the auld Halls settled by the Tyne
in a home the Percies gave them.
Walls a yard deep like a stronghold,
for the proud hill a proud cottage –
and we stayed two hundred years.

The line grew through generations:
six children, nine, then eleven.
Grandmother, the eldest daughter,
a widow at twenty-seven –
sixty years without her husband –
taught me how to live with borders.

When she crossed I could not follow,
but learnt how silent some raids were.
By twenty I knew treachery;
a friend, a sister was stolen
in the dark months of winter
then, after a long siege, my father.

We are never free from borders.
My mother died on an ocean,
shores at its reaches; no fixed limits,
just sea reclaiming then retreating.
The house was empty of all it guarded:
another raid had been unexpected.

We meet now on debatable land –
neither south nor north, but beyond both –
and in those moments everywhere
is full of her – the sky, the sun
as it falls by an open door –
she's before me throughout the house.

In the air I feel her pity
for the way we let rooms trap us;
the need we have to put up walls
and defend them; the fear we make
for each other by warring raids
which haste us to that last border.

When I surrendered their old home
I dreamt one night they all came back,
waved to me, walking down the path –
five generations who had striven
to keep the house their parents left them.
If we can't defend we are forgiven.

Special Delivery

Daddy was tied like a parcel,
paper crept steadily round him;
festive with lilies and crucifix
we waited to fasten the string.

I wanted to try for an angel
but demand is high these days;
cheques are too easy, and the heart
hadn't enough small change.

Daddy was tissue paper;
ink stains smudged his eyes.
The wrapping folded over
but he didn't realise.

His room flapped white and yellow,
settling gold when we walked in,
and the angels sniffed at the window,
on the outside, looking thin.

I packed fine memories round him
as gently as I could.
Love, wrapped untold beside him
for fear he understood.

I could not loose the paper
holding him gagged and bound.
We both struggled against it
but it coiled more tightly round.

The angels, unasked, were refusing
to redirect him home,
so I wrote out the label –
'Daddy – destination unknown.'

Amor Diving
(for my mother)

After the police left, having told me of your death,
I picked up the mail I'd thrown on the table
when I came in. Your card slipped out to be read:
but it's not the words you sent me from Lisbon,
the hopes for a smoother voyage after Morocco,
or even your faithful promise to meet me
which stay most strongly – for I remember
the care you would take to choose each picture,
so that was where I first looked for an answer.

I thought the name on the boat you'd picked, bobbing
in the harbour, was *Amor Diving* – just as ours did
into difficult waters – though it always surfaced.
Later, before I sang them at your service,
I realised the words were *Amor Divino.*
For all our differences, that stubborn thread
I tugged at times and frayed, holds still and strengthens
with every passing day. You are proving to me
that no one will ever love me better, telling me
what neither of us ever managed to say.

The First Week

I have left your lipstick by the mirror,
your shoes on the first three rungs of stairs.
I have watered each fuchsia in the porch:
your cacti are flowering like red hands
reaching into the deep window
I would look through to see you
walking up the path.

Every day I make your bed,
sleep in it every night,
trying to dream you back –
but I can't hear your voice
and you stopped the clock yourself
before you left.

Today I started to open your mail,
rifled clothes for your scent
(which seems to grow stronger),
found the letter you wrote to my father
twelve years after he died.

The old mirror has melted
and run under the door, but you are
safe inside me. I will be your reflection:
out here facing the next thirty years.

Post-natal

Being a midwife, you were different
to other mothers, never fussed. You fed
and calmly cared for three generations
under the same roof.

My father once said he was heart-broken
when you left me in my cot, closed the door,
and told him I'd stop crying once I knew
you wouldn't come.

Lately, like a child, I've woken crying;
hungry to see you, touch you, talk to you.
I think you hear me in some far-off room,
would come now if you could.

We all have a second umbilical cord –
the one we never see, that is of our making.
It feeds comfort from wherever you are now;
do not cut it.

The Day of the Funeral

She was born and died in the same month – May,
chilly as it often is in the north.
In a way I felt I met her at the church,
could sense her relief at being home
after those last eventful weeks.
Clouds threatened as we came out of doors,
climbed into the long, silent hearse,
and followed her finally down the street
where she'd shopped for over forty years.

Out past the houses, banks of blazing gorse
flashed the sun she'd managed to switch on.
I felt her with me, yet outside the car.
At every turn of the road I loved her more,
wanted to cling to that part of her
under the red roses and polished wood;
could imagine her – tense, apprehensive,
tight-lipped – putting up with the whole business;
yet the warmth of her smile was everywhere.

The Other Itinerary

Dying's never easy:
you did the best you could –
sent me a card that arrived
the same day as the news;
made sure I had photos of you
smiling, right up to the last minute;
went out in style at a party –
quickly, quietly – in the calm Pacific.

Now, when your face
comes before me
you are usually laughing.
I feel us smiling together
at the death certificate
signed by the Russian doctor
with its 'Welcome aboard' motto
in the corner.

I worried that we'd finished
your film of holiday photos
taking pictures of the flowers
on your grave – then knew
you hadn't minded: it was
how it ended – the way
we welcomed you home.

Worse was the suitcase
I collected without you
but, even then, you hinted
you didn't really need it.
While others had specified
'being met', for once you'd written
just: 'own arrangements'.

Left Luggage

'You can't take it with you,' she used to say,
reading who'd left how much in the paper.
The house is sold but I dream her in it –
struggling through the door with bags and cases
more substantial than she is – leaving them
abandoned on the floor because there is
nowhere to put them.

Someone has filled her cupboards with their clothes.
I know she searches, but cannot see her;
can feel the frenzy in the air, her sense
of things removed, misplaced, not remembering
how, or why, or when. This is vaster than
all the small forgetfulnesses she'd been
used to while she lived.

It's as if time moved on months when she left,
instead of the two weeks she intended –
so that now she's returned, laden and tired,
her life has been wiped out in her absence.
We've sent her home to Oxfam or auctions;
absorbed it, in fragments, into our own:
allowed her to fade.

But in the dream I feel clearly; hear her
wondering why the telephone doesn't ring,
why a new family has changed her number.
And I can see all their puzzled faces
as, every morning, when they go downstairs,
they trip over more of her discarded
luggage.

July

Watching a different sea
to the one on which you died,
I try locking a curious gull
eye to eye.

I am with him on the roof's edge,
thinking only 'high water'.
Then, 'This time last year
I had a mother.'

It's as if one grief breeds others.
When we reached the cliff path
they'd just found the body.

After you died I felt nowhere was safe
but this familiar place
could have been the exception.

Last night I dreamt you met
the murdered girl, were
trying to comfort her.

It's reassuring to think
you'll go on doing
what you were good at –

but here we are road-blocked,
our walks policed or televised,
the streets subdued, until
our late-night neighbour
starts his 4 a.m. toccata –

and when I sleep again
you have your arm around her,
and you're saying, 'I know,
I had a daughter...'

Gulf

When I wake alone in a drone of planes
it's twenty to five – three nights since you left,
just noise in the sky over someone's roof
as they tried to sleep. These pass, heading east,
their high whine muffled by thousands of feet.
I've dreamt of men, whose minds are drifting sand,
guiding you to airstrips on unknown ground.
In the glare of my lamp dust swirls and gleams,
sticks in my throat as I reach for a drink.
Tomorrow news will flash on TV screens
and, in the moment I'm not looking, you'll
be seen – acting as normal, as if all
this could be over soon – but then my glass
hits the table; it echoes round the room.

Difficult Times

These are difficult times. April arrived
through a rush of rain. In the train window
a newspaper – fingers at either side –
skimmed, superimposed, across a landscape
bereft of houses. A child's charred hand dropped
out of focus – emerged from a long
pool of waste water and was folded up,
left on the seat.
                   We are watching this war
on a faraway screen without the sound.
Nothing seems to matter more than the rain.
As we left that train the city filled with
workers and shoppers, doing whatever
passes for life.
                   The value of pity
sinks slowly in our purses and pockets;
we edge along pavements. In a minute,
someone anywhere might be blown to pieces:
it's all either cowardice or courage.
Daily, new mothers are wielding pushchairs,
thrusting their offspring out, ahead of them,
into the face of oncoming traffic.

Divided We Stand

You are looking at me now like the man from Special Branch
who scrutinised my face when I waited to board the plane.
I thought – somewhere there must be a terrorist with my eyes –
I expected to be stopped. He waved everyone straight through.

I came separate, out of place, through my own act of faith.
You stood among families waiting to be completed –
but I had never promised. Doubts soon sabotaged your smile.
Now we move from room to room switching on and off the lamps.

I wake before dawn. A bang: my bed is scattered with glass –
shards, glimmers, jagged pieces. The floor is sharp, clothes covered.
You fill the doorway, lift me; my feet touch down in your room –
'Keep right back from the window!' – but outside the street is calm.

An empty chair, a towel – your clothes are tidied away.
Only the bed is betrayed, the imprint of your body.
You do not declare your fear, your craving. No crucifix
clings to the wall, yet your eyes are praying into the dark.

At the side of the curtain we peer down to a pavement
which keeps its feet a secret under a stone-blinded lamp.
You are looking at me now as if you hope I'll declare
a shared religion or guilt, something that might help us cry.

The closed door has a halo. Shut out, shut in, it's the same.
You hold me pressed against you; pick the glass out of my hair.

God's Train

'Does God's train stop at Reading?' asked Kevin.
'Would you know God if you saw him?'
Snow blew through the waiting-room doorway.
'Has he changed his mind about resurrection?
Does he look like the Transport Police?'

Fellow passengers shivered on the platform.
When he is too cold in his room, Kevin
shuttles himself between Earley and Bracknell:
no one inspects the ticket in his shoe.
What could I say but, 'I hope so' and 'No'?

The Destruction of Sodom and Gomorrah
(from the painting by John Martin, 1852)

No one ever asks why I looked back.
They all know the story of Lot's wife
who stood stupidly despairing when
she should have fled. It was not like that.

Imagine a great tide of fire
with waves higher than nearby mountains
crashing down, at once, on two cities –
buildings, bodies exploding. The heat.

I breathed in spray of freshly-burnt flesh:
friends, neighbours – my young, married daughters
whose husbands would not heed Lot's warnings.
I'd wanted them to marry herdsmen...

Yet Lot was always a city man,
tolerating our city's ways till
its rabble threatened to rape his guests.
His response? 'Leave them: take my daughters.'

We still had two girls waiting marriage:
'They have not known man; do as you will,
only spare these men under my roof.'
Luckily the strangers intervened –

but after that I would rather have
fed myself to the raging furnace
than follow him. The sun was rising:
eventually I had little choice.

We were out before flames closed the gates,
welded them into the scorching stones:
the sun, smothered in fumes. No strangers
to be seen – only a burning sea

vaporising. I could taste the salt,
feel it crust my fingers; the muscles
of my face tightened. It stung my eyes.
As towers toppled, I became one.

Salt corrodes but I would rather watch
destruction than follow my children
to a desperate future, plying
their father with wine from Gomorrah

until he lies senseless and they claim
his wizened body as their birthright,
taking turns at my place in his bed,
handling him, taking his seed by force –

I noticed the pitchers carried *so*
carefully, the wild plans in their eyes
as he herded them past me. I could
not bear to face the future. Looked back.

Pandora's Daughter

I have kept a spoon
licked by the last woman
to run from the kitchen
when lava leered through a doorway
in lonely Pompey.

I keep all deserted ruins,
abandoned homes,
unanswered prayers.

My box is hinged with sighs.
It expands in the dark
to cover continents.
It shrinks at morning
so you can put it on a shelf
or even in your pocket –
but never in someone else's:
it is always heavy.

I open it constantly,
add sorrow by the shovelful:
the man who married someone else,
the woman who sacrificed herself,
the children who were never born –
all buried under a thousand wars,
millions of unfed mouths,
an avalanche of frozen tears.

I sift them with this spoon
(it is large, like a ladle),
and wish that I could alter
reality to fable;
that I could lose
box and spoon together;

that I could
forgive my mother.

Metaphor

(for Mary Fedden and Strawberry Hill)

At first we didn't notice it was growing dark.
We lit the chandeliers at noon – then earlier.
Sometimes we tripped over furniture:
the gloom cast up a suit of armour.
Each one of us felt the cold iron hand
on our shoulder, some time or other,
crept our way down corridors
which were growing narrower.

Yet it was broad day by the gazebo. Birds sang.
The garden stretched out in the sun
like a woman reclining on a long, curved couch.
Inside, we stumbled, losing our grip on the light.
We saw that this darkness was special to us.
Doorways filled and shrank with shadows.
Sometimes voices called across the tiles
tempting us to jump over the castled edge.

We turned our backs. Then one day
a harlequin ran towards the house.
Clowns bounced down the lawns. Their music
lured a few of us out – for a moment or two.
Not all made it back. (Notice the girl
blowing by the border; the dog, still trying
to leap out of his shape.) We couldn't escape
except back to the dark. Nowhere was safe.

The music took squirrels into the river:
a peacock span round on the highest turret
and disappeared – but indoors, books rustled,
there were glimmers of light: there were the hands.
Hands on the stair-rail below the Library –
ordinary hands with the touch of a mother,
moving together; folding the dark
into long, heavy sheets, corner to corner.

They were all the magic that we knew
against darkness. They shook out shadows.
Gradually we learnt to hear our own music;
learnt to distrust the slick sparkle of clowns.

Rock

The rock had spent thousands of years
on the spot where he had tumbled
when the glacier left him.
The tiny fissure in the earth at his base
became bigger: water seeped into it –
it widened and followed its own course.
The rock watched, always from the same spot.

Men came and went. The rock watched.
He grew tired, weak, felt that every storm
was wearing him down. Even the red ants
were dismantling him, grain by grain.
He had broken himself into boulders
and let them roll away: lichen, thrift,
wagtails' feet persisted. He stopped caring.

One day a woman appeared, gathering ling
and bilberries. The rock saw her, struggling
in the bushes with bedding, brooms, fruit
for her children. She sensed his dilemma,
drew closer, laid her hand against rock,
and passed on her power. 'Endure,'
she said – and the rock endured.

New Wings

Strathieburn

These mornings, you leave the place in darkness –
the hills, nowhere visible;
behind you, a blankness
which might be the wall of a ruin.
It seems the world has returned
its first chaotic moments –
air heaving water
in a howling wind.

This is the time before stone hardened,
was hewn and hoisted,
roofed and roomed.
Everywhere there is movement;
nothing stands as it will when
light fixes leaves on bushes,
branches on trees, the tracks of a fox
across the cold field.

When this happens you will have gone.
But here and now as the wind dies down
you stretch your arm into nothing
and hold on. Somewhere, you hear a word
in the voice of the burn.
The closed door has disappeared:
the track starts at your feet

though you cannot yet see it.

Lifeblood

I remember when I was still hopeful,
would never check the date,
took it for granted – and laughed
at red flashes on the pavement
in the sun as I ran, rushing as usual,
my swirling dress and sandals
jumping them as a child dodges
the cracks between paving.

I still felt young, those last times,
when my body, filled with drugs,
manufactured what it was told.
I bled day after day, unexpectedly;
stopping and starting, my head
drilled by pain. Thick splashes surprised
on a cold stone floor, vermilion-
stained granite; I wasn't prepared.

Nor was I ready to wait at the hospital
for yet another scan, beside expectant mothers,
thrilled with their new knowledge
of the children inside them.
I was glad they had their futures,
could understand their pleasure,
but it increased the pain
of finding more tumours, however benign.

Now, I miss my blood, its new brightness.
How young it seemed, and comforting.
All was well, the cycle completing.
It whispered, 'Not this time, but soon…'
I always thought that when blood
didn't come, a child would,
that when it finally went, I'd be old.

I still feel young, yet am freshly spotless;
cannot pass my blood on, as my mother
did, to me. Safer and sadder now,
I try not to think of all the wombs
they test later, to be able to tell you,
'It was for the best' –
for life – but only your own.

Learning to Read

It wasn't at all like the first time
when my father, tired, and smelling of work,
pulled off his overalls in front of the fire.

He tried to distract me as I pressed him
with my day-old copy of *Robin*,
finally gave in and rushed his way through –

skipping bits (I knew) and winding up
abruptly with, 'So Richard Lion said,
"Go – to – bed." I'm going to get my dinner.'

I knew this was a plot, so I laboured,
peered over pictures, matched them to words,
and struggled letters into sounds.

I remember the moment the first word clicked
into my mouth: my brain yelled, 'Yes!'
The roof lifted off our house.

As I knelt on the red rug in front of the fire
pages were alive as I turned them –
so many voices! It was like watching a film

suddenly break out of freeze-frame
and turn on the sound. I tucked the comic
under my pillow, light as a pair of new wings.

In hospital, nearly forty years later, even a comic
was too heavy to hold, so it wasn't apparent
that I could no longer read, until I came home.

I learnt that will is not enough. Long afternoons ached
the weight of words, taunting with familiar shapes,
dizzily spinning. I lacked strength to wrestle them.

Then my father's tired smile came suddenly to me; his voice
that only speaks in dreams now, laughed gently: 'Go – to – bed.
It'll come like Christmas. You don't forget how to fly.'

Panoramic View

As you sharpened your focus, my vision blurred. Inside,
I re-ran shots of all the worst moments – over and
over – ones I needed to drown in the darkest loch
in preference to being there myself. I'd forgotten
you had picked up my camera the last time we walked
out of the house together, away from unyielding
granite walls, her voice on the answer phone, everything
safe and loving that I'd ever known in our shared life.

From the Hill of Fare to Bennachie, just out of sight,
snow lightens low capped hills and the sun casts a hard glow,
a false semblance of warmth, on frozen ground spreading out
from the Forest of Durris and our house: a solid
clump of chimneys, roofs, walls – braced against unrelenting
cold. Our track is lost: stiff bushes edge the long stretch to
the road. It's a bleak scene softened by three sheep. One looks
at you; another stares at a slight shape by the fence

that would be easy to miss, but memory helps me
recognise myself. I'm set so far in the margin
as to be lost to undiscerning eyes, concealed in
a landscape where I've woken, in my mind, each year since.
The last photo of me I never saw you take, kept
for moments of longing, when weight of your loss left me
in despair – to remind me that, if chance were to let
you find it now, you'd just see sheep, a field, the sun's flare.

Signing Off

At the checkout in Sainsbury's I signed my name –
rather – the name I'd been left, that wasn't mine
now you had gone. It was your name I signed. Both
initials and surname – yours, not mine. Pure chance.
Thirty years ago it was fate, an omen
we were meant to be. I fused my life with yours
quite readily. What's in a name? Hope, love, pain.

Would I sign it again? Something wasn't right.
Of course: you'd left and I'd lost myself, but how
could a stranger know so much? At the third try
he rang a bell. Could I tell them why my hand
shook? Why what I'd scrawled looked nothing like my card?
It was hard. Two pairs of eyes now scrutinised,
as well as the growing queue. I thought of you –

something I'd been trying not to do. No help.
How could I explain I'd thought you were the best
part of myself? When that went, what could be left?
Something I couldn't write. Why wasn't it clear
who I was or where I'd been for all those years?
Suddenly I knew: I'd been you. I needed
my own name – to live again, buy food, survive.

Two Springs

One north is not like another: one flight
north by northeast – under two hours
and I'm plunged back into winter;
snow still patches the dead ground.
The thermometer outside my window
reads two degrees when I mist the glass.

I know there are bluebells in England:
days ago, I walked through them
in a leafy wood. Here, trees are too bare
to imagine leaves – and the only blue
is a ship in the harbour, bigger than
millions of bluebells, blocking out a church
and a run of roofs with its cold bulk –
booming in the night, like a restless animal
taking soundings off Finland or Estonia.

Now we have rain from a grey sky
and the figures on the walkway,
half-way up a hillside, hurry,
walk stiffly, their eyes on the ground,
as if, by staring, they will warm it
and make the grass grow.

I live in eight tiers of single people,
draw the blinds when they do,
turn up the heat, boil a pot
on the stove to make some tea.
The radio tells me there are wolves
still – in Sweden. When the ship
booms again, I think I can hear them
calling down from the north
that winter is ending.

The Swedish Climate

Just yesterday, when the sun surprised us
by acting as if it had always been there,
and managed to trick a whole bed of crocuses
into opening before the middle of May,
we smiled in the streets, shed our ski jackets
and layers of clothing, phoned to say, 'Hej!
Come have a beer. We're moored here in a bar
watching buds burst on the Djurgården trees.'

Today the temperature has dropped by
twenty degrees. Back in our coats, silent
in the rain, then underground, we have
Garbo faces: it's a serious business.
Our profiles lift to the distance.
We do not smile, want to be left alone,
as if we will risk abdicating our country
by riding the subway to New York or Rome.

Tobias and the Angel
(from the painting attributed to Andrea del Verrocchio)

In the pocket of my long, grey coat
Tobias is walking out with an angel
who is taller and broader than he is.
In one hand he grips a small scroll, and a string
which swings a fish along the inside of his thigh.
The angel catches the fish's eye or, perhaps,
what draws down the glance, is
a fingertip on top of that large, pale hand.

Tobias looks up expectantly, but has not yet
learnt a way of touching which is allowed.
His fresh-faced, feminine beauty fails to lift
angelic lids; his cloak, thrown up, makes
an ineffectual wing. He has not yet learnt
the nature of the journey. The angel strides, feet
strung only with the semblance of sandals.

Tobias's finger holds the stride in check:
the angel's red and black plumage rises –
they settle in a corner of my pocket.
In this city of fourteen islands it is easy
to think you are walking on water
at the heart of an archipelago
that has secularised its angels.

By the waters of Strömmen they walk briskly
along Kungsträdgården, taller than I am.
Gliding down a stairway through rock and water
to a train gusting light out of the darkness,
then staring from stained, faded seats –
any angels seem stranded on the surface.
What is the nature of the journey?

Roused by the movement of a fellow traveller,
I look up into a face that has no features.
Scars pucker in uneven pigments; eyes flit
to the exit for Valhallavägen. A downward glance,
coat flapping free as we begin to rise,
that large hand resting near to mine.
I reach out, but have not yet learnt
a way of touching which is allowed.

Leonardo's Dog

Born outside marriage, he learnt to challenge
authority, tradition, rules that could stop
a man seeing past his horizon into
the future – Verrocchio's apprentice in
a city of silkworkers and palazzi,
a teenage dandy with a passion for flight.

Struggling to the suburbs with cages of birds
he'd bought to release, Leonardo watched them
beat freedom back into their wings; they flashed
across the fields. He'd been allowed to finish
the wings of an angel at Christ's baptism,
but nothing was as beautiful to him as these.

When Verrocchio entrusted him with Tobias'
fish, the one killed to cure his father's blindness,
each brushstroke caught its final gasp; the last thrash
of its tail shimmered in the air as if Tobias
had just slipped out its entrails for a magic potion
and popped them in the box pored over by the Angel.

His master pleased and everything accomplished,
he could have left it there, but a fish, however
recently killed, is still a dead fish. Alone with
his little white dog, jumping and rolling, Leonardo
saw suddenly, at the Angel's feet, those
lively black eyes, a translucent coat trotting.

Cacti and Love

I knew the desert without driving to it:
the road went straight through my forehead.
Fat branch stumps of Joshua trees,
like a cross between a cactus and a palm,
stopped a long way short of the clear deep sky.

Cacti reminded me of my mother –
difficult to touch without injury to each other.
But when she was happy, relaxed, no tensions,
her smiles were exotic, unexpected flowers.
Her cacti bear with me and still blossom.

We both needed love: I still need it now,
and hope is everywhere in a desert –
cacti bloom; light lifts us into its space.
We forget alien distance, the lack of water:
cacti and love outlive their owners.

For Eileen

(In memory of Julia Bassler, 1967-97
and William Bassler, 1968-1990)

We wade to the abandoned farm
thigh-high through grass and September flowers,
reaching into boughed-down nettles
to grasp the warm weight of apples.

Only bears and blue jays come to feed –
the chimney fallen, the hearth cold.
No one harvests; no one ploughs;
their horses are dead now, or grown old.

We leave the apples to fall and sprout,
begin a descent past the squeaking tree,
and sit on cool earth at the top of the slope,
backs to dry trunks, feet one with roots.

Below us the caves; below them, your farm
where dog sniffs frog around the pond
and groundhogs visit the empty barn.
Asters straggle. The beavers have gone.

You carry the weight of autumn with you,
won't let it fall, fear what it will seed.
Apple boughs can be eased of fruit,
but all the bears in this state can't devour your grief.

        *   *   *

Beyond our sight, her cubs shadow the she-bear;
never leave her. Our young
reach out to us on their own terms.

Spring brings the circus to New York –
not across bridges, or up 42nd Street
beneath 'WALK' and 'DON'T WALK' signs –
but in the dark through a dimly-lit tunnel,
hundreds lining deserted night roads.

First, swaying trunks disperse the cold – then,
cantering riderless out of the darkness,
horses whinny to a human herd.

Try to hold on to that night you waited –
to life the city held out, like a ripened fruit,
letting your sixty years slip underfoot
as you ran, shoulder below steaming shoulder,
one with them in a clatter of hooves.

Dream Lore

The night before last, I set out to find my mother
but my purse had been stolen and she'd moved away.
Last night she hugged me in an empty room
where she'd just made a fire. She threw on years
like logs. Some took a while to catch and flare
but when they did we had time on our hands.

It was so good to be back in our old home
though the furniture had gone and a new family
was unpacking underneath a window
thrown open to the street. My mother and I
were happy just to be together. 'Don't worry,'
I told her, 'I'll work as long as it takes to keep you warm.'

Years whistled and spat; the children came over
to warm their hands. Someone closed the window,
opened the door. My mother was smiling. She'd wrapped
the boy in my father's scarf and the girl in an old coat
of her own. When she hugged me I knew I could always
find her here, sit down with her, reach into her arms.

Meeting again after almost eight years.

How can I tell you? Are there enough ways
so that you will not see too much of the pain,
so that I will seem as I would like to be again –
a woman with life singing in my veins?
Love that can be reckoned is a passing craze.
Ours held more than either of us could explain
and even though you've left while I remain,
it's love that heals the hurt through every phase
of learning how to live a separate life.
Now years that should have drawn us together
pass between us like a broadening river. I've
no time for regret, though loss has its costs – never
doubt that I remember our best hours, or was the wife
who once said, 'No one will love you better.'

50s Jive

Eight men stand by the door, hugging their pints,
watching the floor. You ask them to dance – en masse.
No one says 'Yes'. One thinks about it…
When you were growing up, men asked women. Now,
we do it ourselves if we want it to happen.

You hang around, drink, watch the band.
Then, when you're about to move on, one
reconstructed Elvis nods and grabs your hand,
spinning out and back into a right-hand catch.
Palms press, push you off into turn after turn.

He pulls you back; you have to follow
though he hurts your arm, is too controlling –
but it took so long to get him going that
you don't want to give it up so easily.
After a while you rise above the aching,

fall into the way he always leads,
get used to him treading on your feet.
Until someone younger, bored with her partner –
a pushy, fast foot-worker – puts herself
between you two, and he lets himself

take her, leave you. He's whisked away
out of control: you're suddenly freed,
relieved – move to the door. But before
you go through it, they start arriving –
young men who really know about dancing…

Kiss

Her feet felt beautiful in the rain
that seeped under straps and over soles
while the steps in San Marco overflowed
and lanes poured costumes in the flood.
Down every alley and canal
they floated, fixing masks in place –
laughing, drinking, making love.

Alone, and not expecting love,
she'd heard the music of the masks,
indistinct voices without mouths,
long before faces put them on.

So now, as she launched into the throng
and heard his voice speaking her name,
asking, one by one, until he came
so close, his warmth surged down her back –
although she turned, her mask in place,
and he asked if she was herself, to her face –
she would not reply until their mouths met
and he recognised her lips for himself.

The Attachment

You always click with a virtual man.
He knows the right keys to press for instant release
that flashes up time and time again.
He's fast, but holds his text in check
and just when you think he'll let it all go,
your screen squeezes for a second
and then, the flow
shoots line after line
in a fluent burst
of explosive words
and you both have
a poem.

Music of the Hemispheres

In such a November night as this,
wind flings rain against the glass
behind closed blinds, and the light
in which your fingers tap, travels on
half a world to my sunrise.

You write from tomorrow:
I read it today, reply,
then sleep as you move towards noon.
Soon I will wake as you go home –
your day ended, mine just begun.

Often, you write to me round noon,
words which travel as I sleep at 2 A.M.
Our minds linger to meet outside time
in a space we create, that is always light,
where bodies break orbits and gently collide.

Wildfire

'Stay warm in my arms,' you wrote,
and their safe warmth gathered me in.
If I try hard I hear your heart
as strongly as you once felt mine
pulsing through a glow of skin.

It's been months since we could touch,
months before we'll meet again.
The bush is lit with burning chains
that ring and choke your summer air:
I shiver in December rain.

Yet in the dry husk of the night,
I remake myself in flame
to leap across a hemisphere
as if the seas were river-wide
and deserts only forest tracks.

I need to know that you are safe.
The warmth you made has kindled such
an intense heat, it cracked the case
and freed a seed sprung from us both,
to grow where fire-winds let it root.

The trees here stiffen white, asleep.
With you, they burn. Trunks, fizzing sap,
fall on each other in eager flames.
Reach out your arms across charred ground:
these fires will pass, but we will not.

Mnemonic

(after Pablo Neruda)

So many nights I could not rest
because I loved him, and sometimes he loved me too.
Then he loved her, and sometimes he loved me too.
I could not rest because I loved him
so many nights.

When I touched him I feared rejection.
Because he loved her, I should be nothing to him.
So many nights we loved, and she was nothing to him.
Did he remember this
when I touched him?

I did not hate her because she loved him –
but not as I loved. Did he remember this?
I could not rest until I touched him.
He scorned rejection:
I did not hate her.

When we met, the hill was empty.
We sat alone. I still remember this.
I did not touch him because he loved her.
Would I hate her
when we met?

The waterfall on a steep hillside
was only sky between the trees.
It was nothing to us. We sat alone.
The sky flowed:
the water fell.

Because he loved her, I would be alone
unless he loved me too: I rejected this.
Remembering, he could not rest –
yet did not touch me
because I loved him.

Like water, he could not rest
because he loved her, and sometimes he loved me too.
Touch should be nothing to us. So many nights
flowed between
like water.

Remember this: the steady flow of sky
numbed the pain of the whole hill-side.
We touched like water then, no hate between us.
I hope we both still
remember this.

Dreamcatcher

was in dry dock, sailing nowhere.
If we *could* pursue dreams
on any navigable ocean,
what would we find there

but embryonic visions
in shadow on the surface –
of insubstantial, shifting,
shrinking dimensions –

they'd be of little use.
Dreams need to grow
and when do we let them?
There's always an excuse,

yet from birth they hover
round us. Babies fist
the air to seize them;
grips loosen. We grow older.

It's an instinct we're born with
and, at first, we fulfil it because
we're not too ambitious – warmth,
soothing sounds, a smile, a kiss,

light, sweet tastes, bright shapes –
all this is easy if they want to give.
But as we cross the mark, time
and time over, it takes

everything we've got to keep afloat:
we're low in the water, dragging
so much dead past with us
it can fill the whole boat.

We can't see what we need to cast
over the side for our dreams to swallow
until they're big enough to catch *us* –
wrench the rudder from our grasp.

The Kiosk, Constanta

It was warm for October so she had the door open.
From the counter, she could see a young man
walking straight towards her, well dressed – foreign.

He didn't run, though there were seven, all starving.
They leapt at his pockets, but he didn't glance down
or brush them off. Could he be her only customer all day?

She'd loved their own dog when they lived in a village:
each house had a cow and they grazed them together.
There was ground for growing, a garden; fences

for protection: gone in a wave of a dead man's hand.
They'd been swept into the city like so much rubbish,
into rooms without land, couldn't keep her son's puppy.

Last year he was bitten outside their apartment.
Strays were usually too weak for aggression,
but this one was desperate for food. She couldn't afford

the best treatment, never brought him here. Parks
were for dogs, lost, like theirs – hundreds of thousands –
with jutting bones, missing feet, eyes like old men pleading.

The young man burst in, breathless, couldn't speak Romanian,
picked up the best chocolate and held out a note.
It was so huge she couldn't begin to change it.

City Bride

She is late.
Every sun-bleached stone
rising ledge upon ledge
to the narrow stretch by the Cathedral door
waits.

She is late.
Guests congregate above
the square, like seabirds
finding footholds on a crowded
cliff.

She arrives
and scales the steps
in impossible shoes
with a smile that lifts the spire even
higher.

She sings.
White flowers float like
feathers from her hair.
A warm tide washes time through the
door.

She speaks.
The blessing ends:
bells clang an ancient tone
against the ringing of her mobile
phone.

Something Bigger

It was the tenth of September, nine in the morning.
I'd followed twelve strangers along a metal catwalk
high above the Rocks in Sydney Harbour, the only
part of this that made me giddy. Glancing through a blur
of boots, down to roofs below and, suddenly, water,
I thought of the Quayside back home, the way everything
is smaller – the Tyne narrower, so many bridges
lined up, one after another. We used to believe
that, for years, nowhere else had a bigger single span
than our green bridge across the Tyne that still turns heads as
trains cross the river. But she wasn't unique, except
to us. No one mentioned the North-East as I climbed, though
these bridges shared more than steel and design.
                                    Headphones told
how sixteen workers died. We'd been breathalysed, asked if
we felt depressed, dressed in shell-suits, sent onto a meshed
gantry, latched on by a slight line to the bridge's rail,
pressed hand over hand up ladders to stand far above
hotels, offices, the wings of the Opera House,
busy water, eight lanes of termite-like rush-hour cars
and lorries thudding, trains vibrating beneath our feet.
The Aussies didn't steal our thunder – their design came
first, was sent over to Middlesbrough where, contract signed,
someone probably pictured it spanning the harbour
and thought how good it would be to have one 'of wor own'.

1924: part way between our two world wars –
the year planes first circled the earth; Greenwich signalled on
the hour; Doris Day, Lauren Bacall, and my mother
first took breath. Seventy seven years later, I stood
a-top an arch while, on the other side of the world,
minds on a mission, making last minute arrangements,
had synchronised a plan into motion – not to build
bridges but to break them. Most have forgotten Sydney's
inspiration: Hell Gate, New York – first, but now smaller.
Build a bridge or attack a culture; those who fall will
be workers feeding themselves, their families. We need
to keep climbing high enough to see in perspective:
we need to keep on stealing each other's best bridges.

Through-lines

Every poet has a subject and mine's survival –
an old woman clutching a naked loaf of bread,
fighting off the dogs jumping around her while
she crosses a road as if under hypnosis.

An old woman clutching a naked loaf of bread –
our small acts of survival shrink to insignificance.
She crosses a road as if under hypnosis:
trucks and buses swerve to avoid her.

Our small acts of survival shrink to insignificance.
The two-hour widow risks shelling to go to her children:
trucks and buses swerve to avoid her.
Not knowing whether she'll find them alive,

the two-hour widow risks shelling to go to her children.
She wouldn't say she has courage, just an instinct.
Not knowing whether she'll find them alive,
a child searches in rubble for her parents.

She wouldn't say she has courage, just an instinct –
fighting off the dogs jumping around her. While
a child searches in rubble for her parents,
every poet has a subject and mine's survival.

NOTES

Isabelle of France (31)

Isabel/le or Isabella of France (1389-1409) was the daughter of Charles VI. She married Richard II in 1396, when she was seven years old, and became a widow in 1399. Henry IV refused to allow her to return to France until 1401. In Shakespeare's play she is not portrayed as a child.

'This music.../ blessing on his heart that gives it me,/ For 'tis a sign of love; and love to Richard/ Is a strange brooch in this all-hating world.' William Shakespeare, *Richard II* (V.v. 61-66)

Kith (35)

In 1138, David I, King of the Scots, moved the Scottish border down to the Eden and the Tees so that Britain was divided into two almost equal parts. At one time Northumbria stretched as far as the Firth of Forth and Cumberland was part of the Celtic kingdom of Strathclyde. For much of the 11th century Northumbria alternated between Scotland and England as the border moved and Scottish kings paid homage for Tynedale intermittently for more than two centuries. The present border dates from the 13th century.

Gruoch (40)

Gruoch was directly descended from Kenneth III of Scotland (murdered by Malcolm II to secure the throne for his grandson, Duncan). She married Macbeth *c.* 1032, either when she was pregnant with her son (Lulach) by her first partner, Gillecomgain, or soon after his birth. Lulach succeeded to the throne in August 1057 on the death of Macbeth (who slew Duncan and was, in turn, killed by Duncan's son, another Malcolm). In 'Gruoch Considers', having taken stock of her situation, she argues herself into the second marriage with Macbeth.

The Swedish Climate (74)

Djurgården is pronounced *yoor*-gordon.
In the 1933 MGM film, Greta Garbo played Queen Christina of Sweden who, in her life, abdicated to Rome for reasons that have never been ascertained. In the fictionalised film, Christina follows her lover, a Spanish ambassador. The last stanza alludes to Rouben Mamoulian's famous final shot of Garbo, as Christina stands like a figurehead at the prow of the ship leaving Sweden, knowing that her lover is dead. Garbo, herself, left Sweden to live in New York.

Tobias and the Angel (74) and **Leonardo's Dog** (76)
The painting, *Tobias and the Angel*, attributed to Andrea del Verrocchio (*c.* 1473), is in the National Gallery. The details of the fish and the ghostly white dog (possibly his own pet) are thought to be the early work of the young Leonardo, who was Verrocchio's apprentice.

Something Bigger (91)
The Tyne bridge, designed by Mott, Hay and Anderson, was conceived in 1924 and opened in 1928. Its design was based on that of the Sydney Harbour bridge, and it is often forgotten that the Australians were, in turn, inspired by the Hell Gate railway bridge in New York, begun in 1912 and completed in 1916. All of these bridges feature twin towers at each side of a steel-arch span.